What is Kumon?

Kumon is the world's largest supplemental education provider and a leader in producing outstanding results. After-school programs in math and reading at Kumon Centers around the globe have been helping children succeed for 50 years.

Kumon Workbooks represent just a fraction of our complete curriculum of preschool-to-college-level material assigned at Kumon Centers under the supervision of trained Kumon Instructors.

The Kumon Method enables each child to progress successfully by practicing material until concepts are mastered and advancing in small, manageable increments. Instructors carefully assign materials and pace advancement according to the strengths and needs of each individual student.

Students usually attend a Kumon Center twice a week and practice at home the other five days. Assignments take about twenty minutes.

Kumon helps students of all ages and abilities master the basics, improve concentration and study habits, and build confidence.

How did Kumon begin?

IT ALL BEGAN IN JAPAN 50 YEARS AGO when a parent and teacher named Toru Kumon found a way to help his son Takeshi do better in school. At the prompting of his wife, he created a series of short assignments that his son could complete successfully in less than 20 minutes a day and that would ultimately make high school math easy. Because each was just a bit more challenging than the last, Takeshi was able to master the skills and gain the confidence to keep advancing.

This unique self-learning method was so successful that Toru's son was able to do calculus by the time he was in the sixth grade. Understanding the value of good reading comprehension, Mr. Kumon then developed a reading program employing the same method. His programs are the basis and inspiration of those offered at Kumon Centers today under the expert guidance of professional Kumon Instructors.

Mr. Toru Kumon
Founder of Kumon

D1307360

What can Kumon do for my child?

Kumon is geared to children of all ages and skill levels. Whether you want to give your child a leg up in his or her schooling, build a strong foundation for future studies or address a possible learning problem, Kumon provides an effective program for developing key learning skills given the strengths and needs of each individual child.

What makes Kumon so different?

Kumon uses neither a classroom model nor a tutoring approach. It's designed to facilitate self-acquisition of the skills and study habits needed to improve academic performance. This empowers children to succeed on their own, giving them a sense of accomplishment that fosters further achievement. Whether for remedial work or enrichment, a child advances according to individual ability and initiative to reach his or her full potential. Kumon is not only effective, but also surprisingly affordable.

What is the role of the Kumon Instructor?

Kumon Instructors regard themselves more as mentors or coaches than teachers in the traditional sense. Their principal role is to provide the direction, support and encouragement that will guide the student to performing at 100% of his or her potential. Along with their rigorous training in the Kumon Method, all Kumon Instructors share a passion for education and an earnest desire to help children succeed.

KUMON FOSTERS:

- A mastery of the basics of reading and math
- Improved concentration and study habits
- Increased self-discipline and self-confidence
- A proficiency in material at every level
- Performance to each student's full potential
- A sense of accomplishment

▶▶ GETTING STARTED IS EASY. Just call us at 800.ABC.MATH or visit kumon.com to request our free brochure and find a Kumon Center near you. We'll direct you to an Instructor who will be happy to speak with you about how Kumon can address your child's particular needs and arrange a free placement test. There are more than 1,400 Kumon Centers in the U.S. and Canada, and students may enroll at any time throughout the year, even summer. Contact us today.

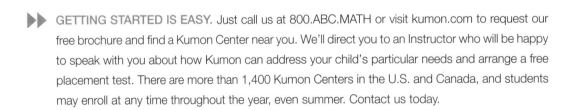

FIND OUT MORE ABOUT KUMON MATH & READING CENTERS.
Receive a free copy of our parent guide, *Every Child an Achiever,* by visiting
kumon.com/go.survey or calling 800.ABC.MATH.

Where Is My Mommy?

Name

Date

To parents Enjoyable connect-the-dots activities are on odd-numbered pages. It is okay if your child draws shaky lines at first; his or her fine motor skills will improve. Ask your child to guess what is shown in the picture. (The answers are at the end of this book.) For extra fun, your child can also color the pictures.

■ Draw a line from 1 to 70 in order while saying each number.

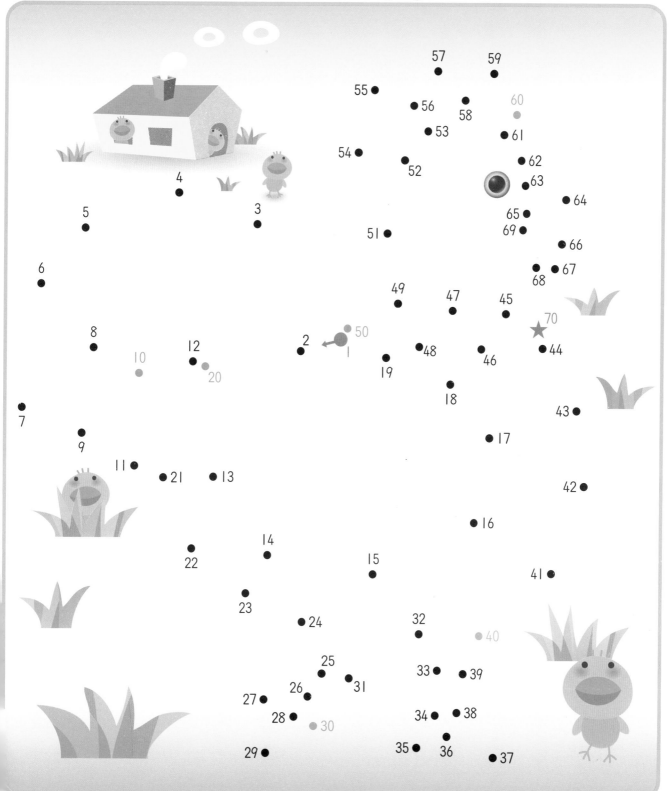

What Is It?

To parents On even-numbered pages are color-by-number activities. If your child has difficulty finding the numbers, please point them out. Praise your child as he or she finishes each activity.

■ Use the key below to color by number.

61 = red   62 = green

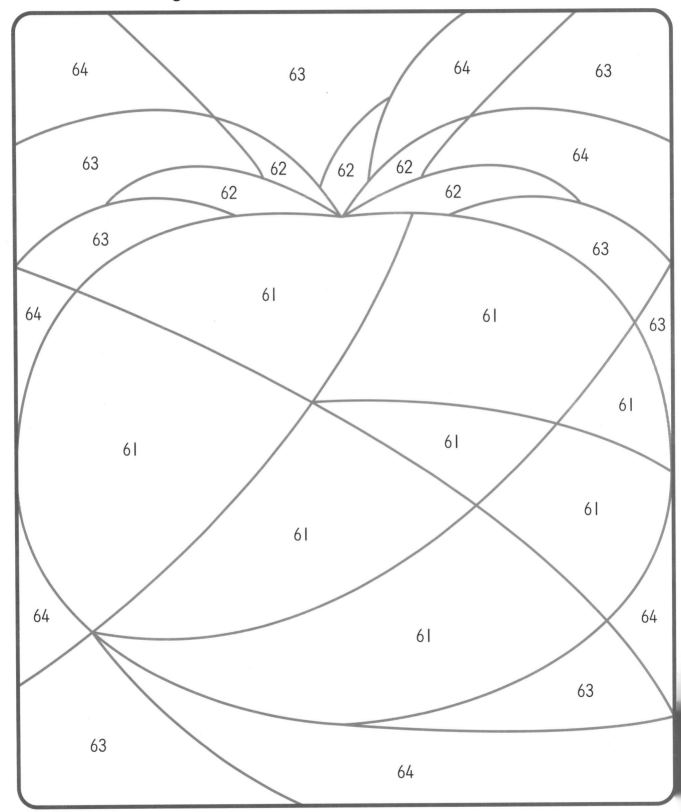

2 I Can Catch Very Well!

■ Draw a line from 1 to 70 in order while saying each number.

What Is It?

■ Use the key below to color by number.

65 = violet (purple)　　66 = blue

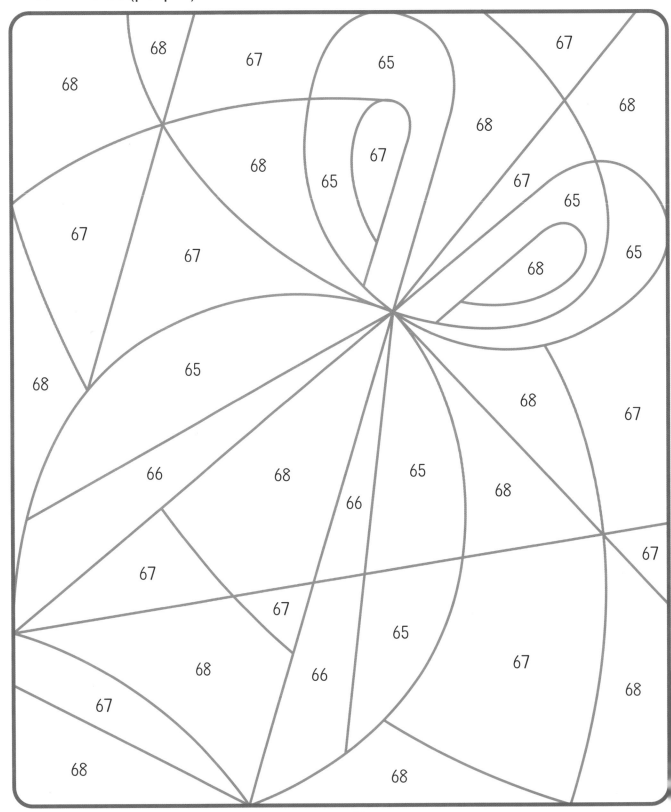

4

Let's Go!

Name

Date

■ Draw a line from 1 to 80 in order while saying each number.

What Is It?

■ Use the key below to color by number.
  7I = yellow green   72 = brown

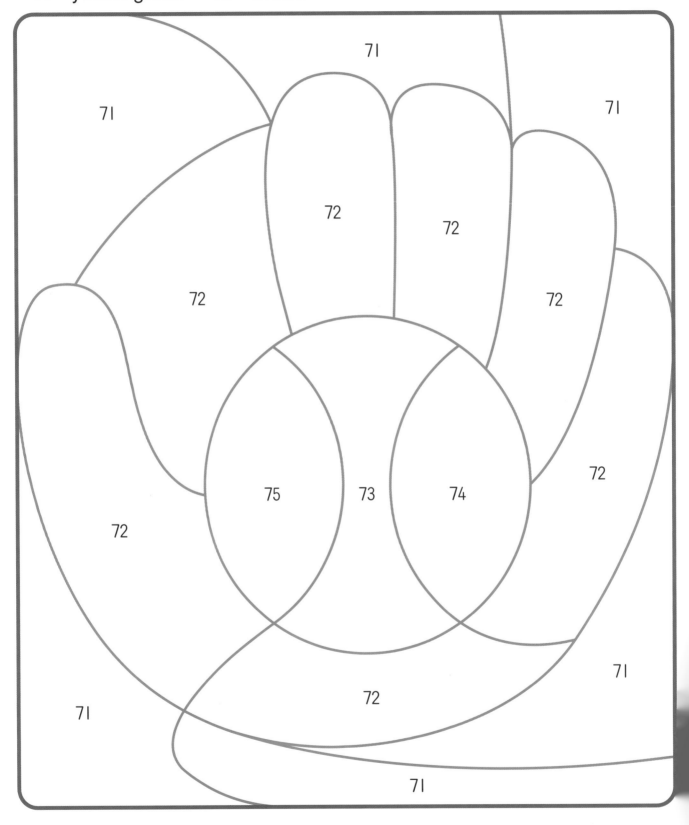

You Are Too Close!

Name

Date

To parents On this page, the numbers become more difficult to find. It may be difficult for your child to draw straight lines especially when the next number is farther away. If your child has difficulty drawing the lines, please offer to help.

■ Draw a line from 1 to 80 in order while saying each number.

What Is It?

■ Use the key below to color by number.
73 = violet (purple)   74 = yellow   75 = black

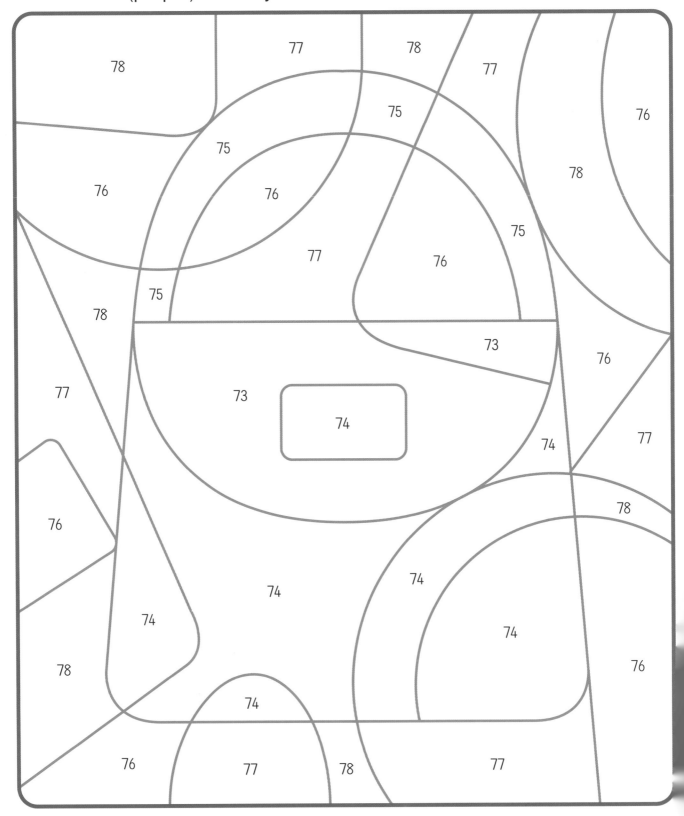

8

5

The Age of the Dinosaurs

Name

Date

■ Draw a line from 1 to 80 in order while saying each number.

What Is It?

■ Use the key below to color by number.
  75 = red   76 = yellow   77 = brown

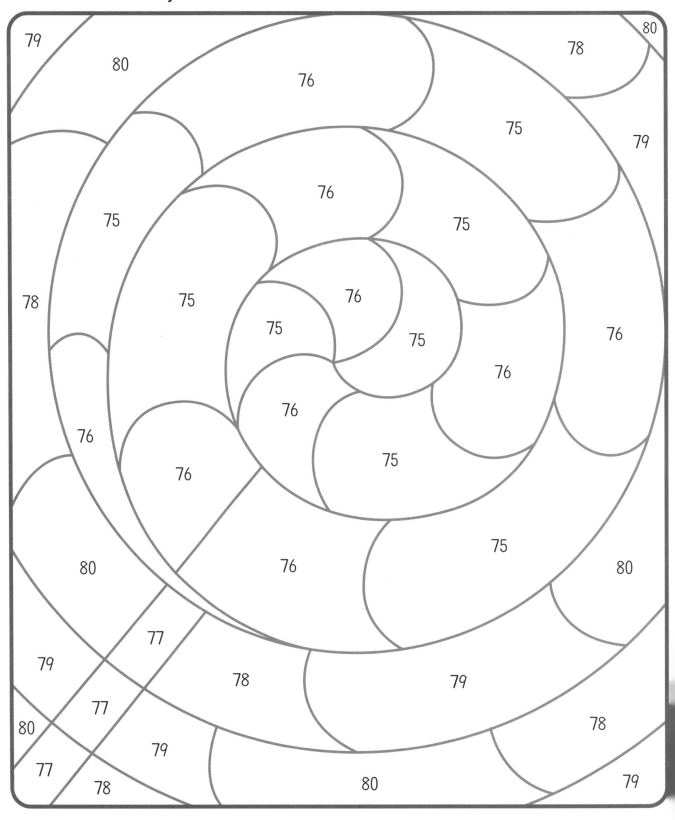

6 Under the Sea

Name

Date

■ Draw a line from 1 to 80 in order while saying each number.

What Is It?

■ Use the key below to color by number.
78 = red orange   79 = black   80 = green

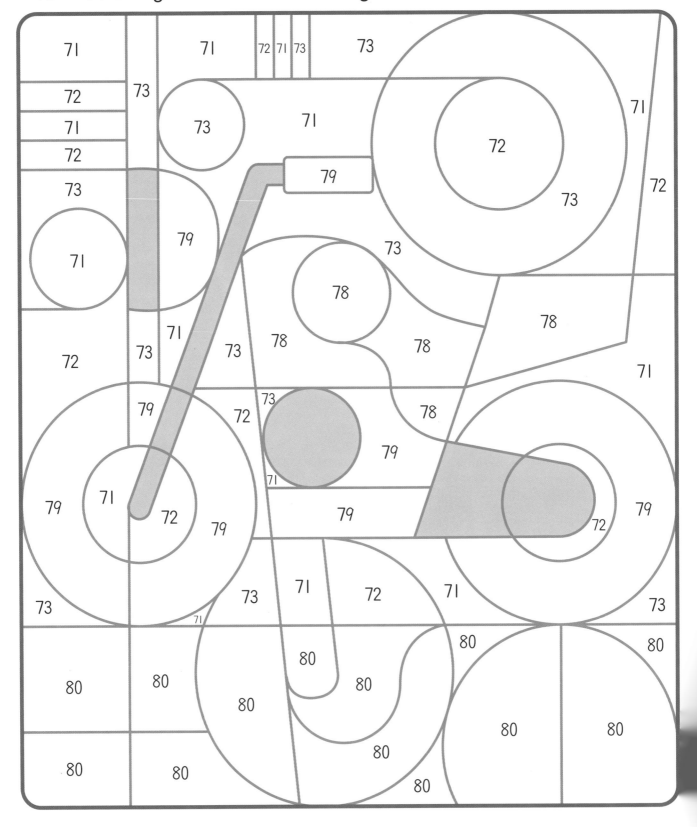

Is It a Penguin?

Name	
Date	

To parents On this page, your child will have to draw many lines that cross other lines. If your child has difficulty finding the numbers, please point them out. Praise your child as he or she finishes each activity.

■ Draw a line from 1 to 80 in order while saying each number.

What Is It?

■ Use the key below to color by number.
71 = red   74 = red violet   77 = black

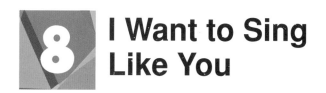

I Want to Sing Like You

<table>
<tr><td>Name</td></tr>
<tr><td>Date</td></tr>
</table>

■ Draw a line from 1 to 90 in order while saying each number.

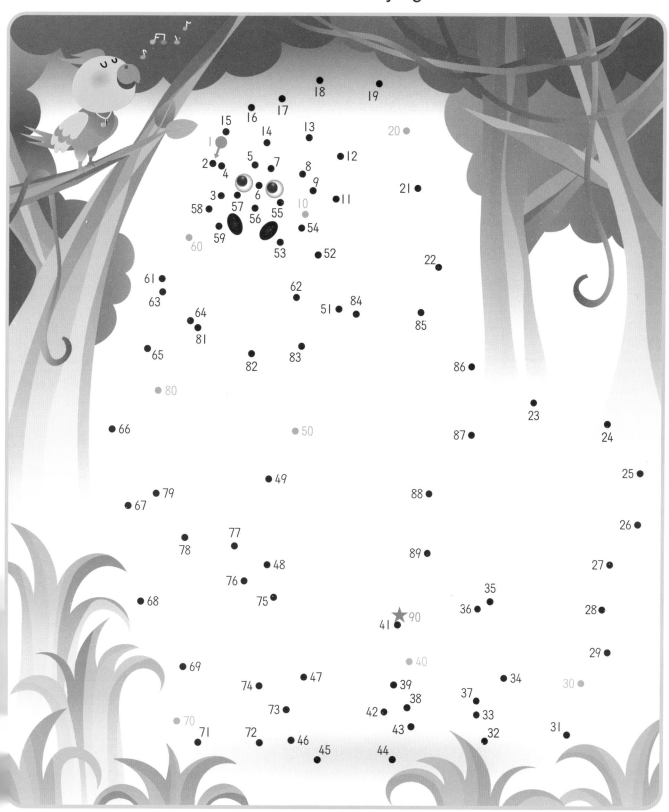

What Is It?

■ Use the key below to color by number.

81 = black   82 = red   83 = red orange

I Like This Fruit

Name

Date

■ Draw a line from 1 to 90 in order while saying each number.

What Is It?

■ Use the key below to color by number.
83 = black   84 = green   85 = yellow green

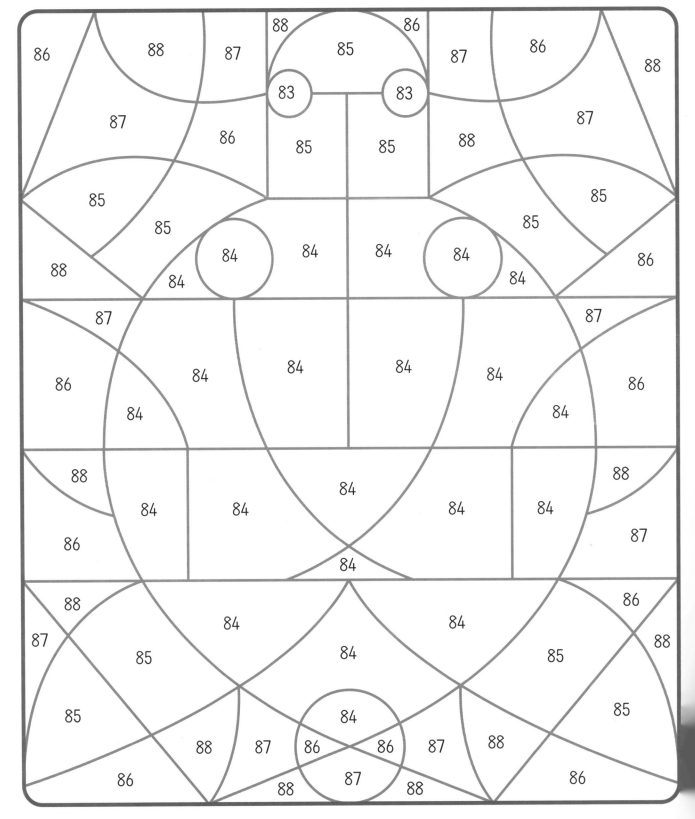

18

Name

Date

To parents From this page on, the numbers become more difficult to find. It may be difficult for your child to draw straight lines especially when the next number is farther away. If your child has difficulty drawing the lines, please offer to help.

■ Draw a line from 1 to 90 in order while saying each number.

What Is It?

■ Use the key below to color by number.

86 = yellow　　87 = orange　　88 = carnation pink

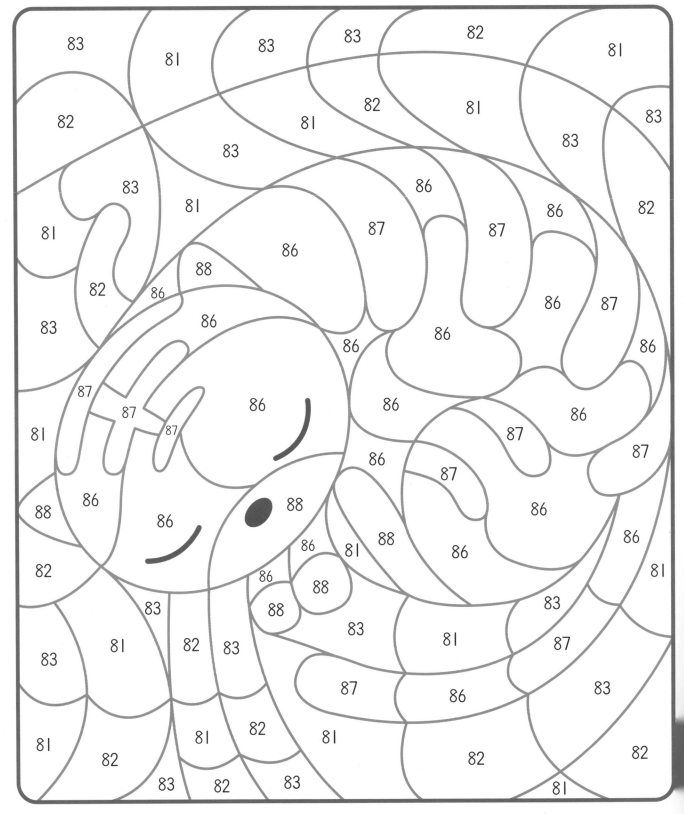

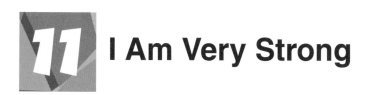

I Am Very Strong

Name

Date

■ Draw a line from 1 to 90 in order while saying each number.

21

What Is It?

■ Use the key below to color by number.
88 = blue   89 = orange   90 = blue green

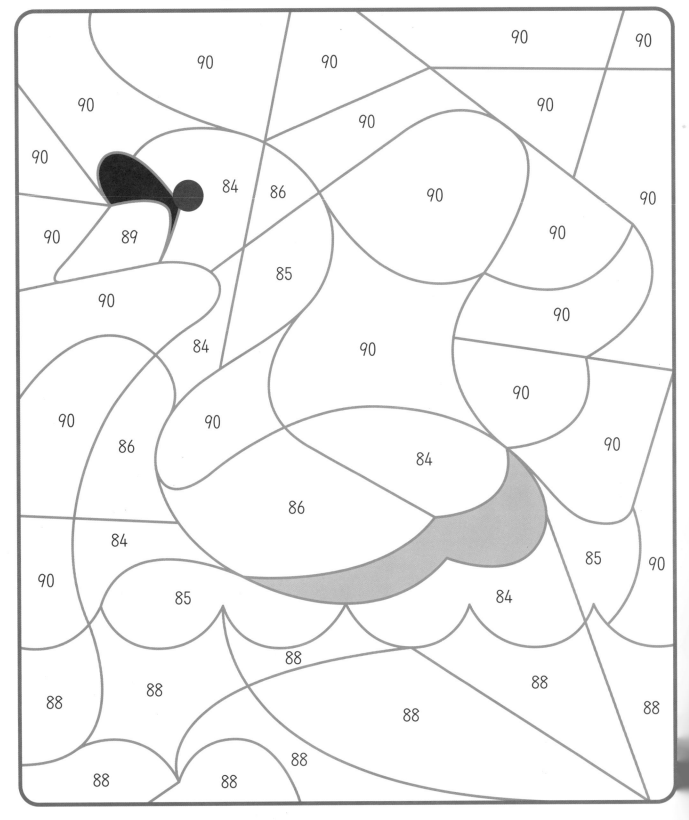

Let's Go on a Cruise!

Name

Date

■ Draw a line from 1 to 90 in order while saying each number.

What Is It?

■ Use the key below to color by number.
  82 = yellow   85 = orange   90 = green

24

I Can See Many Things!

■ Draw a line from 1 to 90 in order while saying each number.

What Is It?

■ Use the key below to color by number.
84 = yellow   87 = orange   89 = blue green

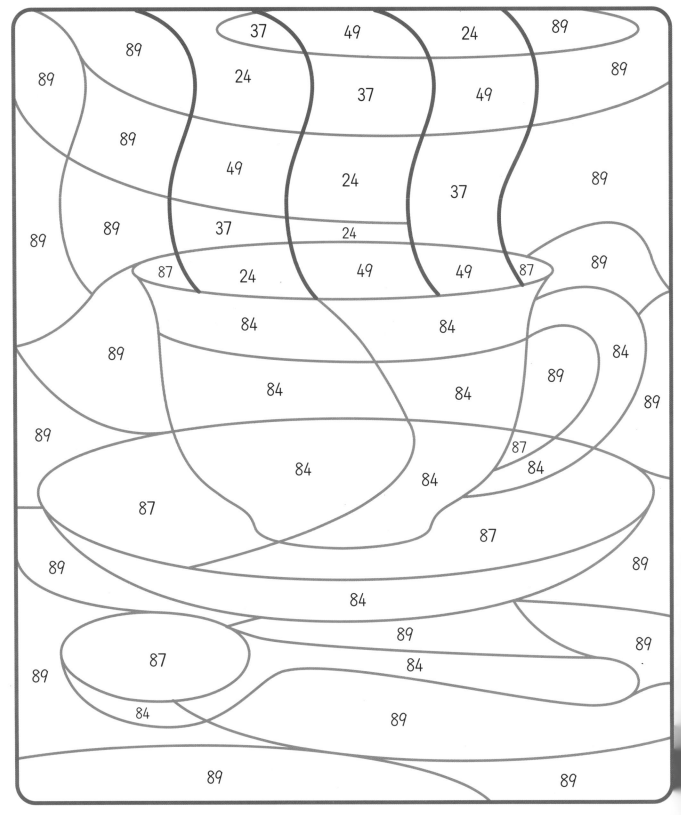

In a Grassland

Name

Date

■ Draw a line from 1 to 100 in order while saying each number.

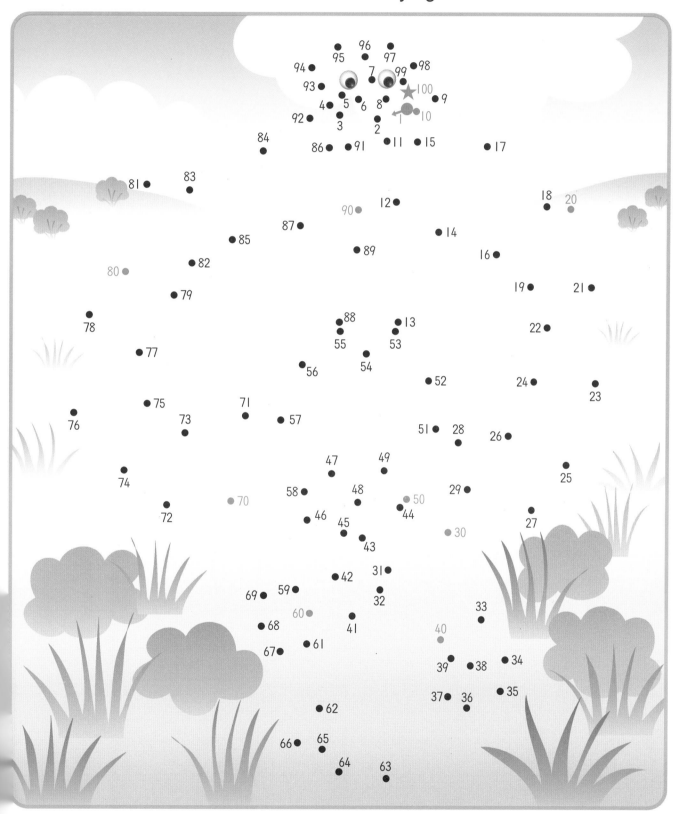

What Is It?

■ Use the key below to color by number.
91 = black   92 = yellow   93 = brown

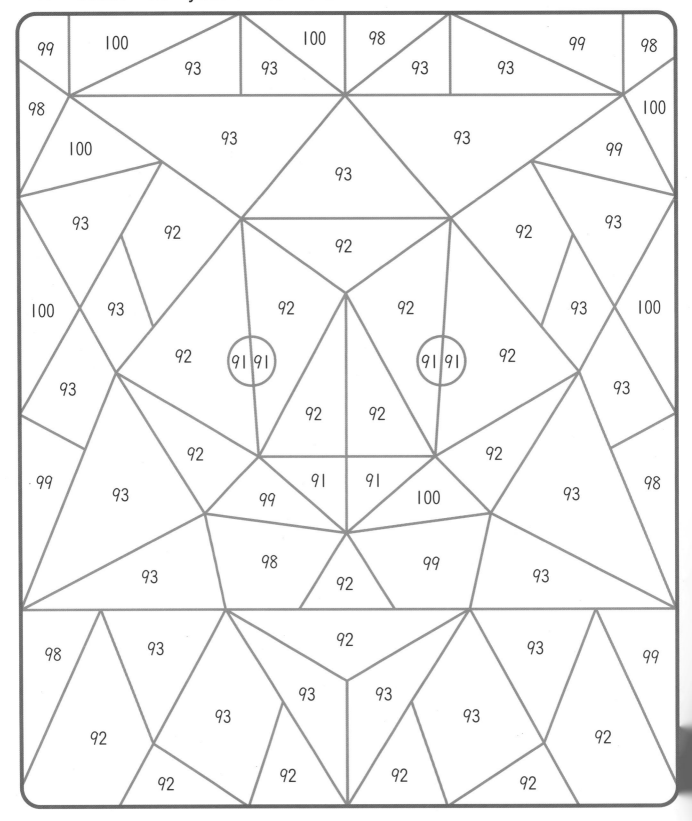

15 Polly Wants a Cracker

Name

Date

■ Draw a line from 1 to 100 in order while saying each number.

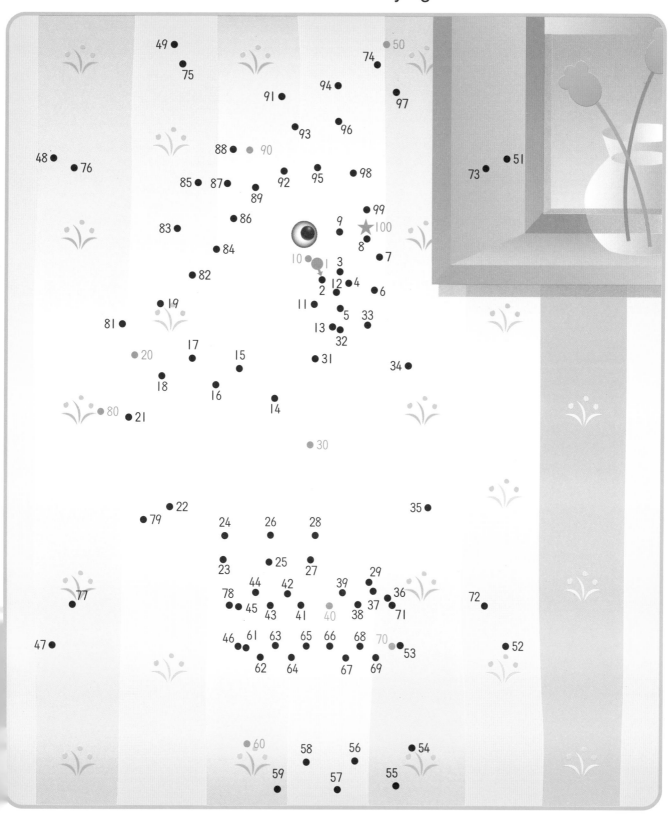

What Is It?

■ Use the key below to color by number.
94 = green   95 = yellow green   96 = yellow

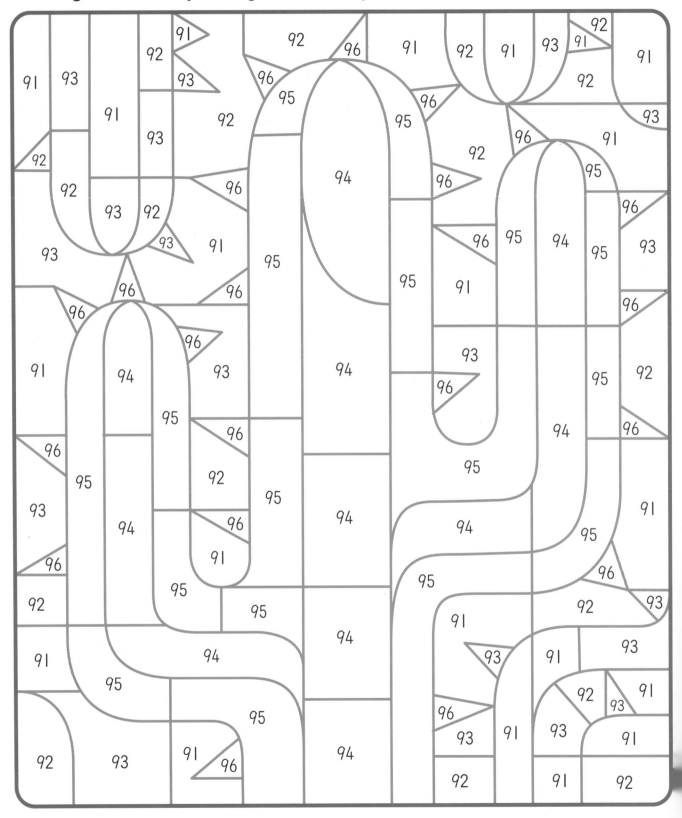

30

Where Is My Hat?

■ Draw a line from 1 to 100 in order while saying each number.

What Is It?

■ Use the key below to color by number.
  97 = yellow   98 = yellow green   99 = green   100 = blue

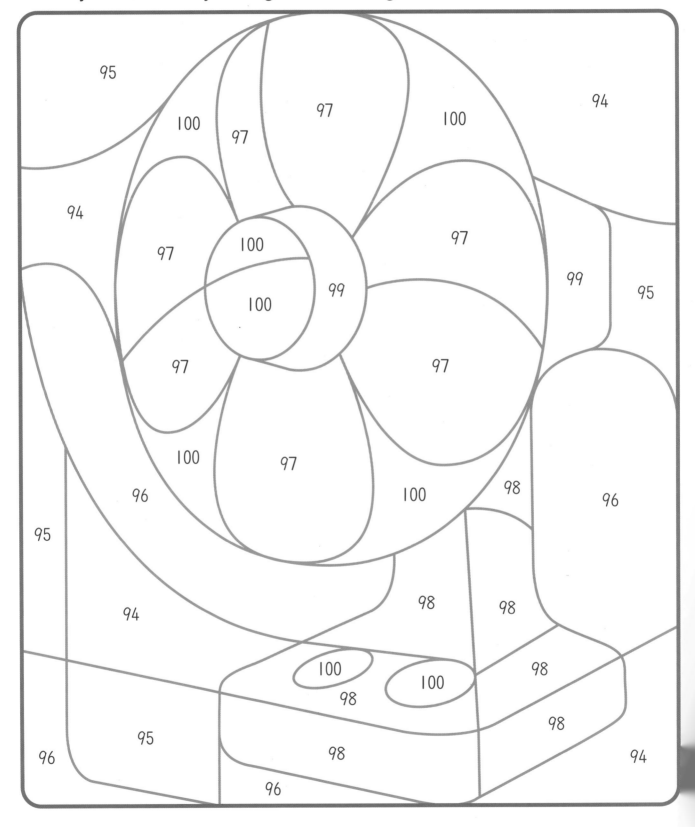

32

I Can Catch the Fly

Name
Date

■ Draw a line from 1 to 100 in order while saying each number.

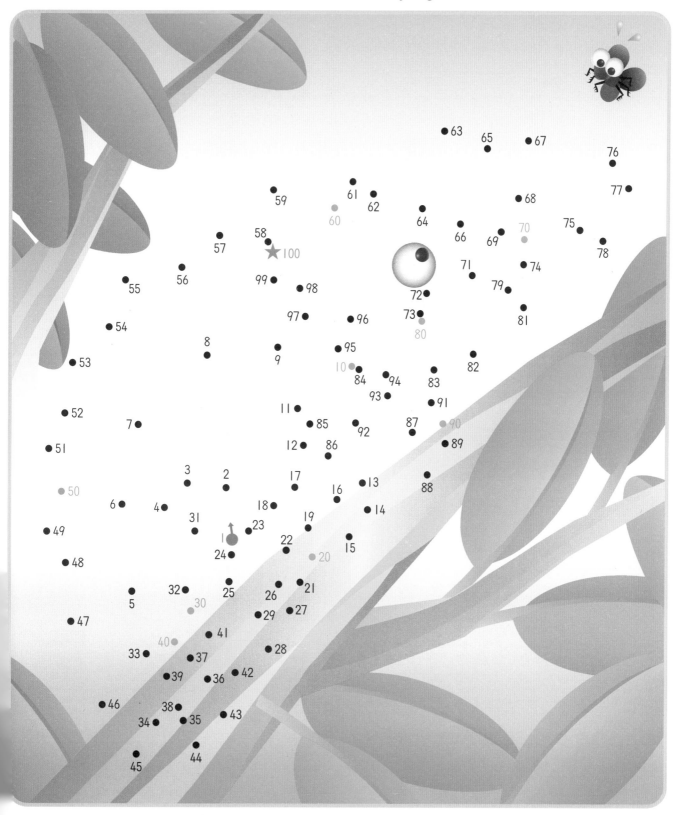

33

What Is It?

■ Use the key below to color by number.

91 = yellow orange   96 = carnation pink   99 = blue green   100 = blue

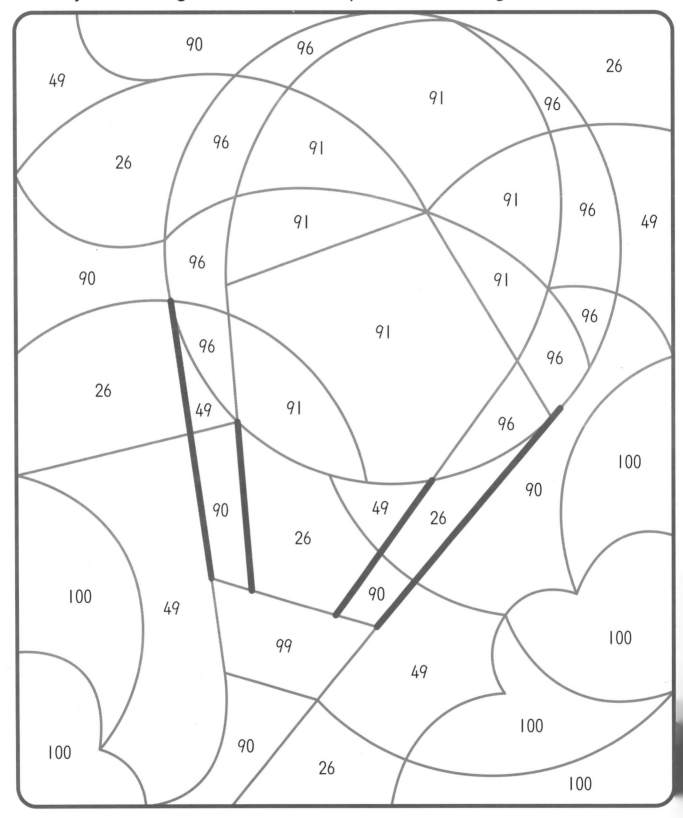

18 A Big Hit!

Name

Date

■ Draw a line from 1 to 100 in order while saying each number.

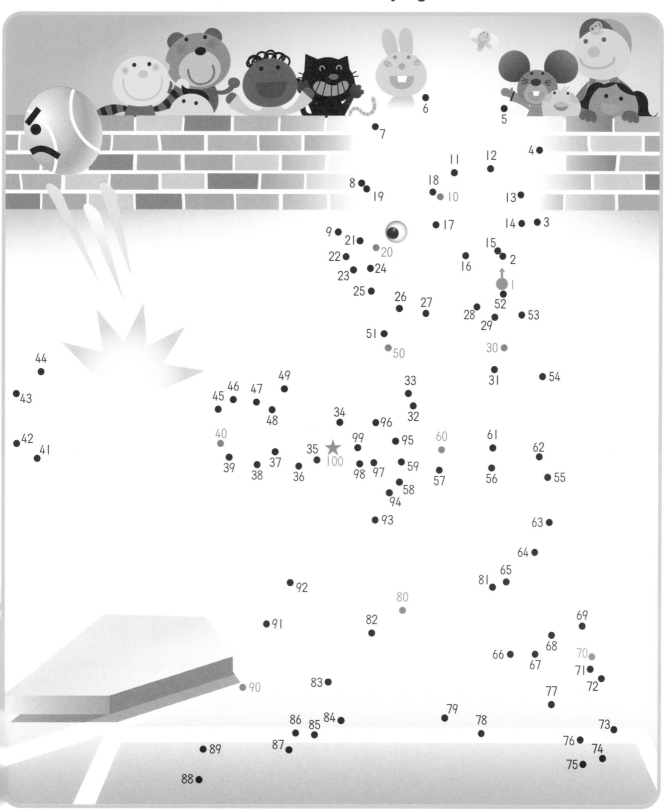

What Is It?

■ Use the key below to color by number.
92 = red   94 = red violet   97 = yellow   98 = blue violet

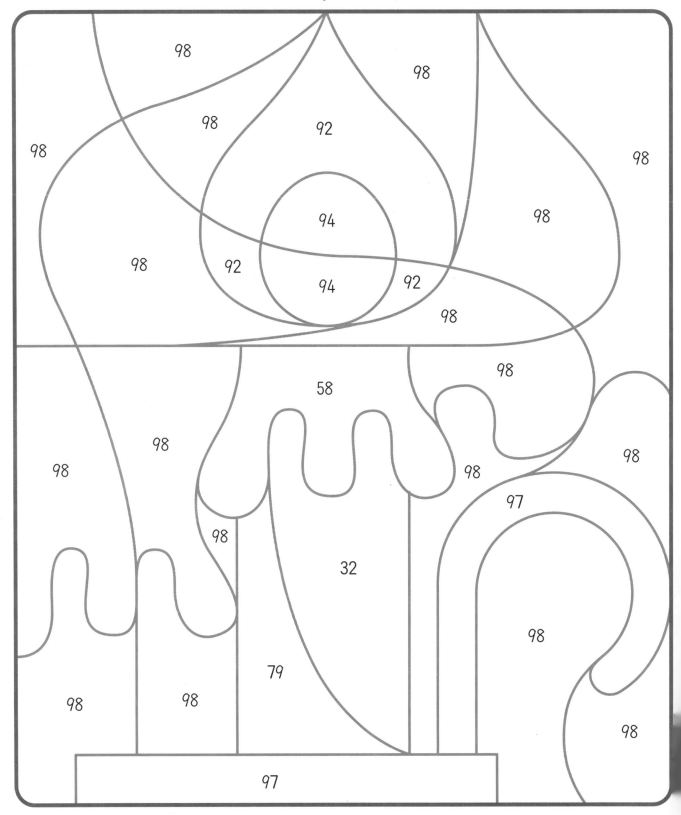

Name

Date

■ Draw a line from 1 to 100 in order while saying each number.

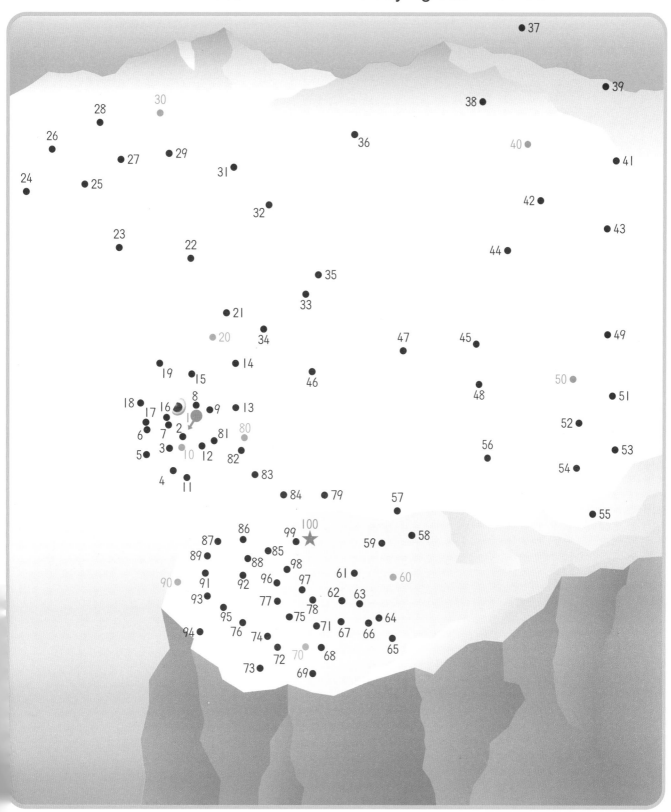

What Is It?

■ Use the key below to color by number.

93 = blue   95 = yellow   96 = violet (purple)   99 = black

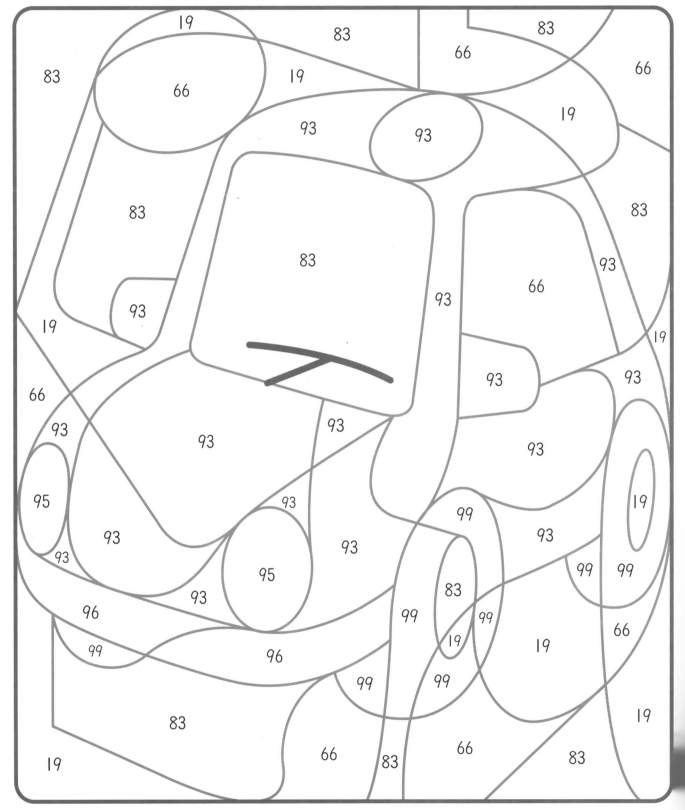

20 How Big You Are!

Name

Date

■ Draw a line from I to I IO in order while saying each number.

39

What Is It?

- Use the key below to color by number.

  101 = brown   102 = yellow orange   103 = yellow   104 = yellow green

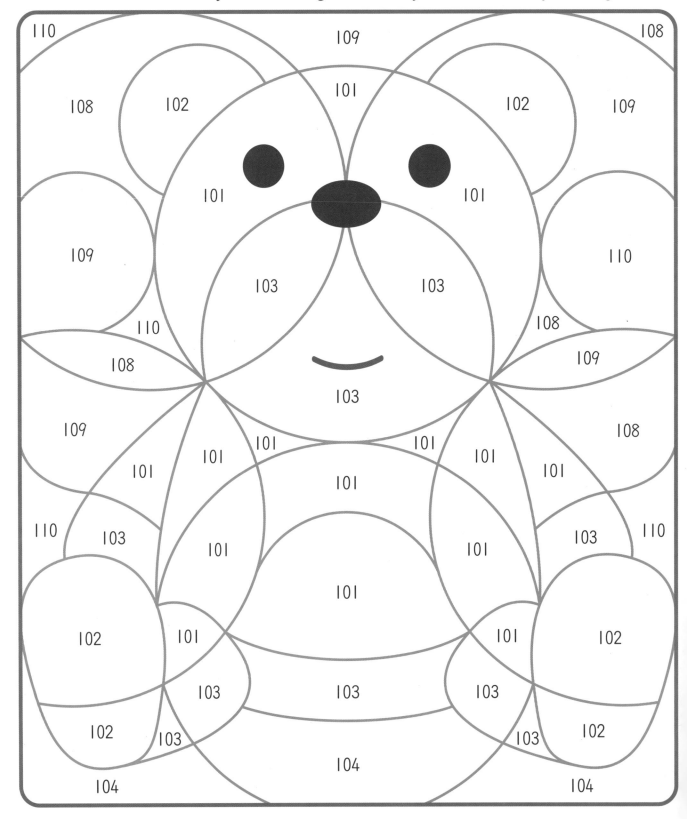

40

Do You Want a Ride on My Back?

Name

Date

■ Draw a line from 1 to 110 in order while saying each number.

What Is It?

■ Use the key below to color by number.
   105 = blue   106 = black   107 = carnation pink   108 = blue green

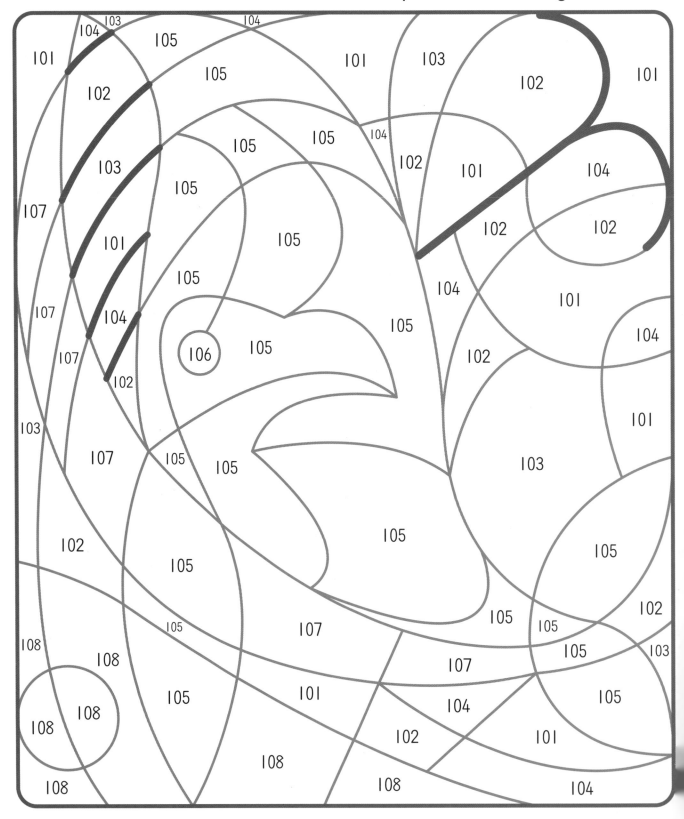

42

Name

Date

■ Draw a line from | to ||0 in order while saying each number.

43

What Is It?

■ Use the key below to color by number.
107 = yellow green   108 = yellow orange   109 = carnation pink   110 = blue

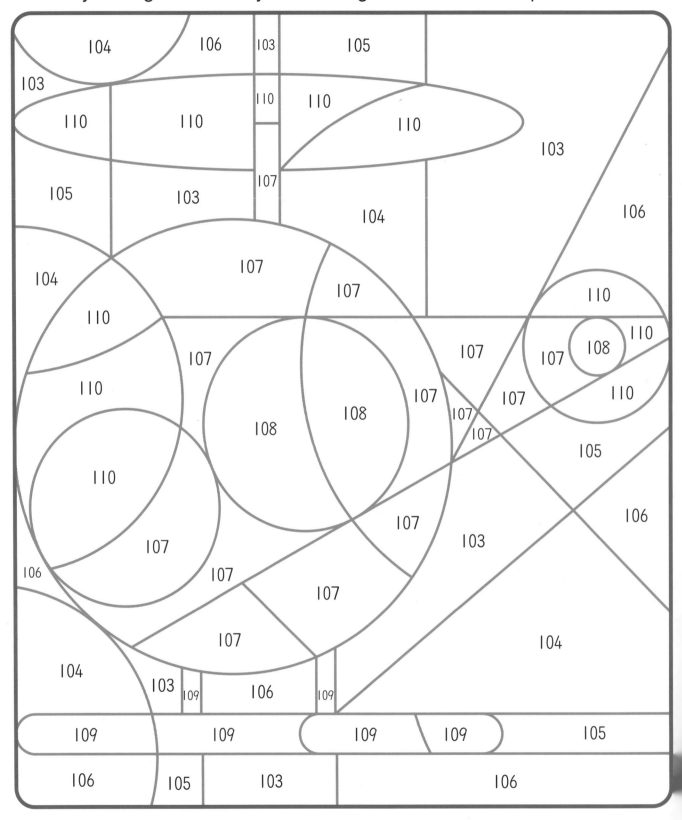

Let's Mix It Up!

Name

Date

■ Draw a line from 1 to 110 in order while saying each number.

45

What Is It?

■ Use the key below to color by number.

101 = black   103 = brown   106 = green   110 = blue green

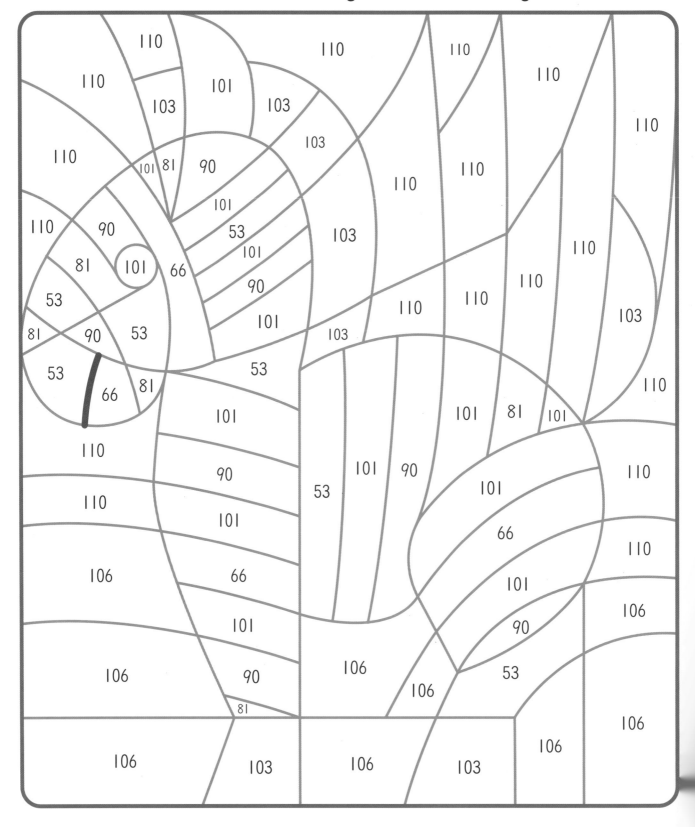

On a Winding Road

Name

Date

■ Draw a line from 1 to 110 in order while saying each number.

47

What Is It?

■ Use the key below to color by number.
102 = violet (purple) 104 = blue 105 = brown 108 = yellow 109 = black

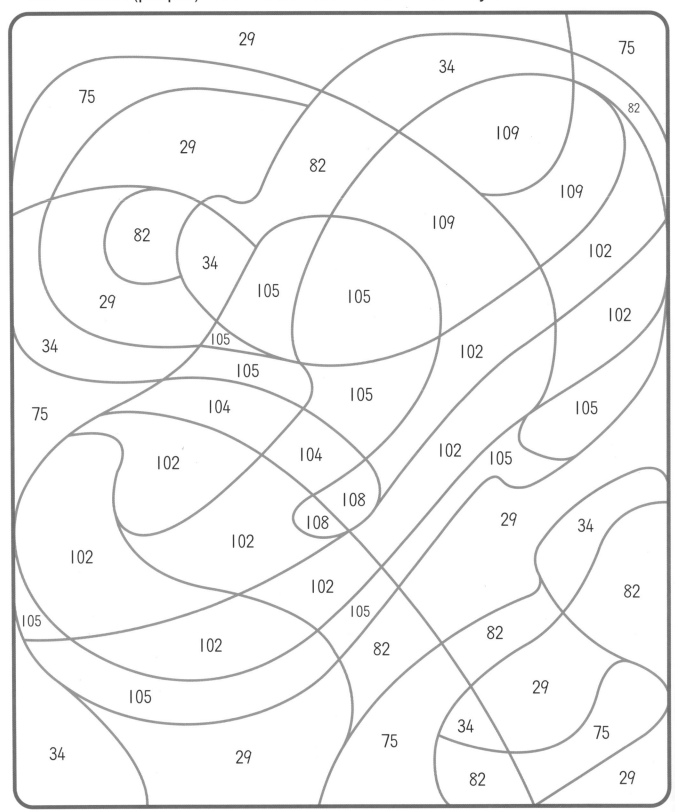

I Like This Horse

Name

Date

■ Draw a line from 1 to 120 in order while saying each number.

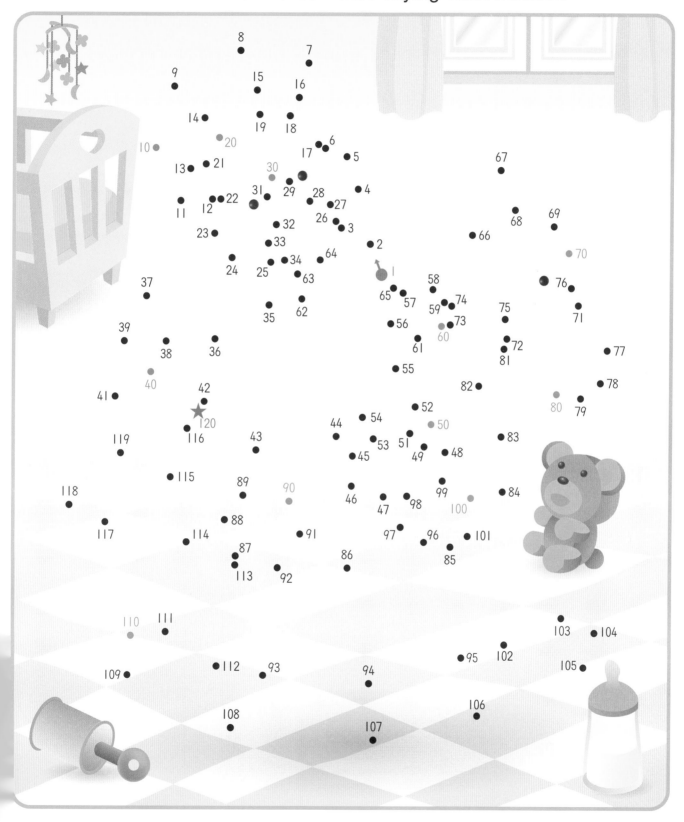

49

What Is It?

■ Use the key below to color by number.
   111 = yellow   112 = black   113 = blue   114 = violet (purple)   115 = orange

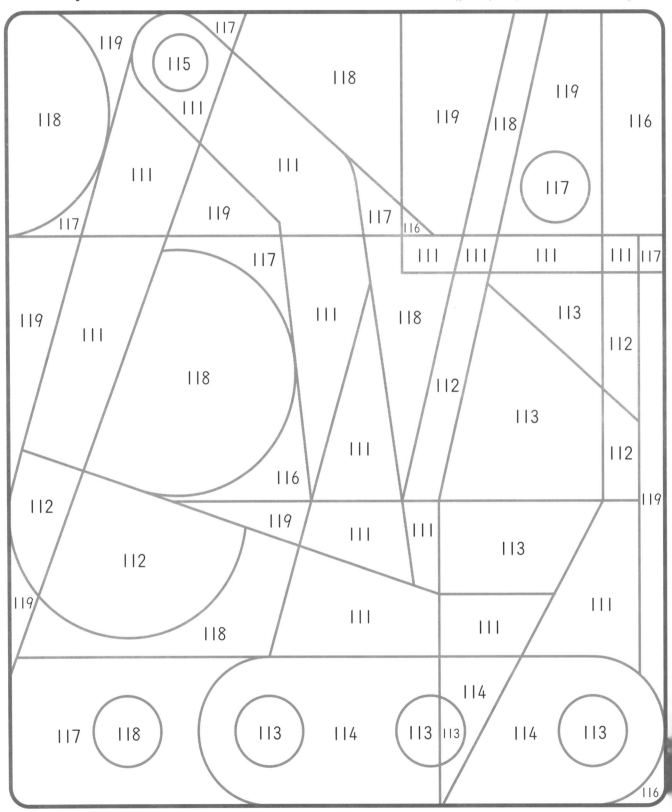

50

Space Walk

Name

Date

■ Draw a line from 1 to 120 in order while saying each number.

51

What Is It?

■ Use the key below to color by number.

116 = red   117 = black   118 = yellow   119 = blue green   120 = blue

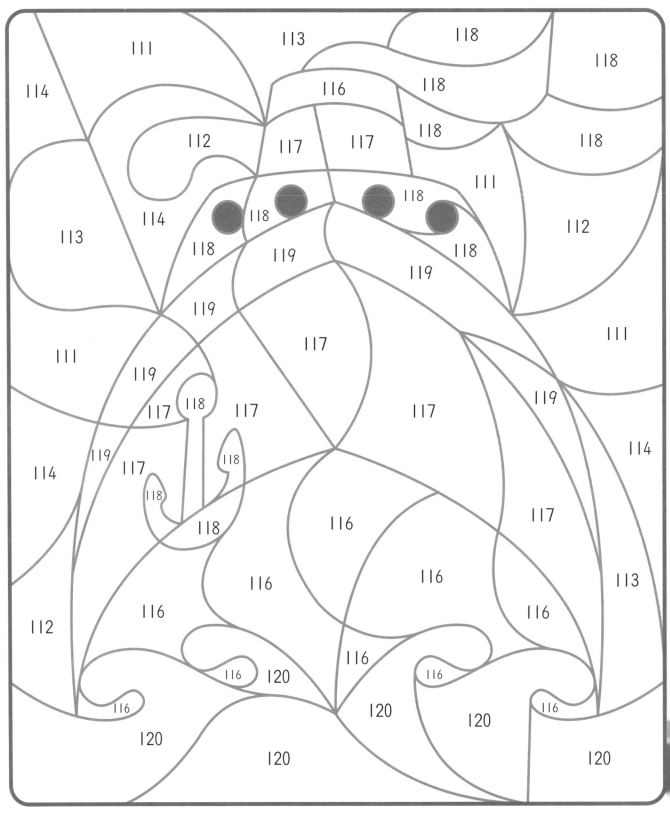

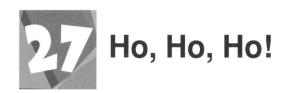

27 Ho, Ho, Ho!

Name

Date

■ Draw a line from 1 to 120 in order while saying each number.

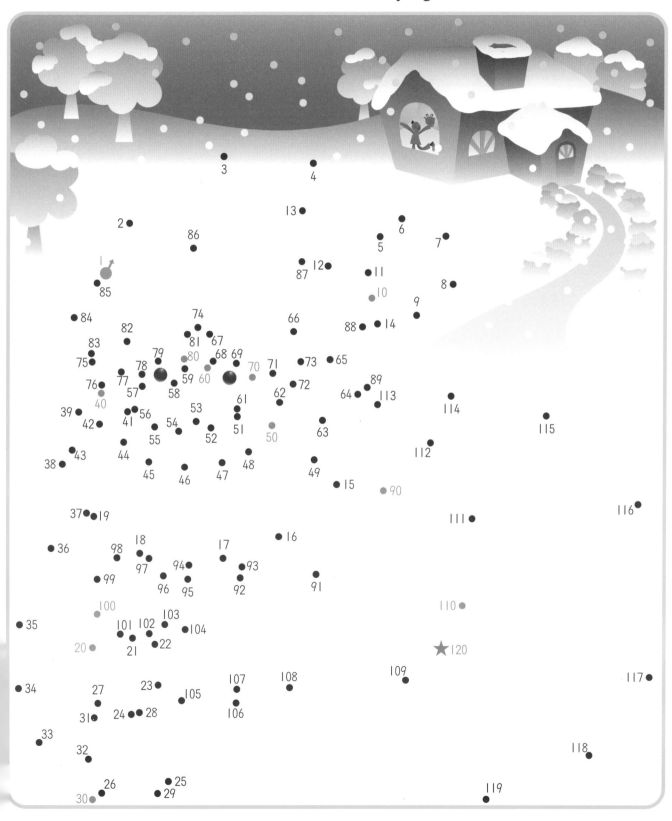

What Is It?

■ Use the key below to color by number.
111 = orange   112 = red orange   115 = yellow   118 = black
120 = blue green

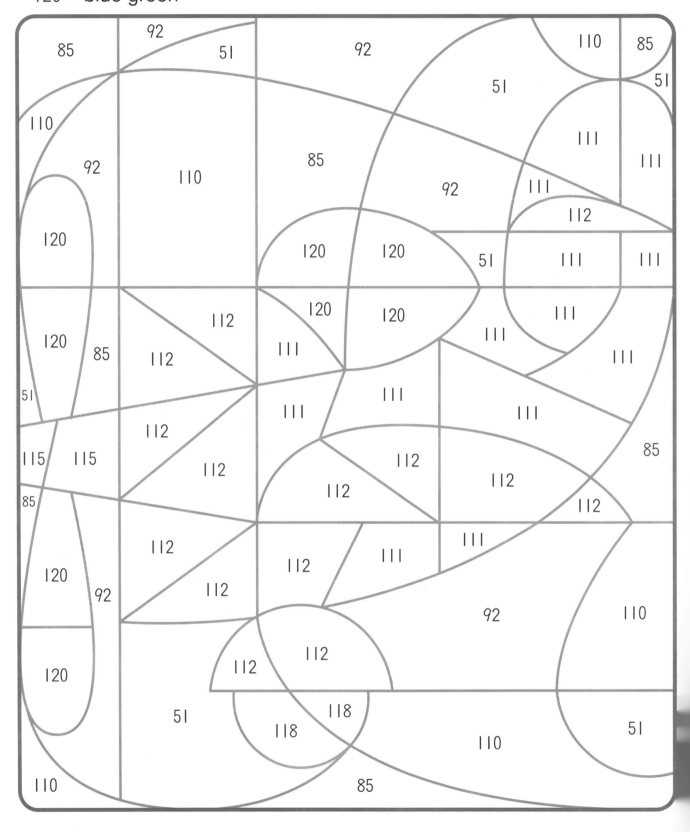

54

Did You Call Me?

■ Draw a line from 1 to 120 in order while saying each number.

What Is It?

■ Use the key below to color by number.

113 = black   114 = red   116 = yellow   117 = brown   119 = yellow green

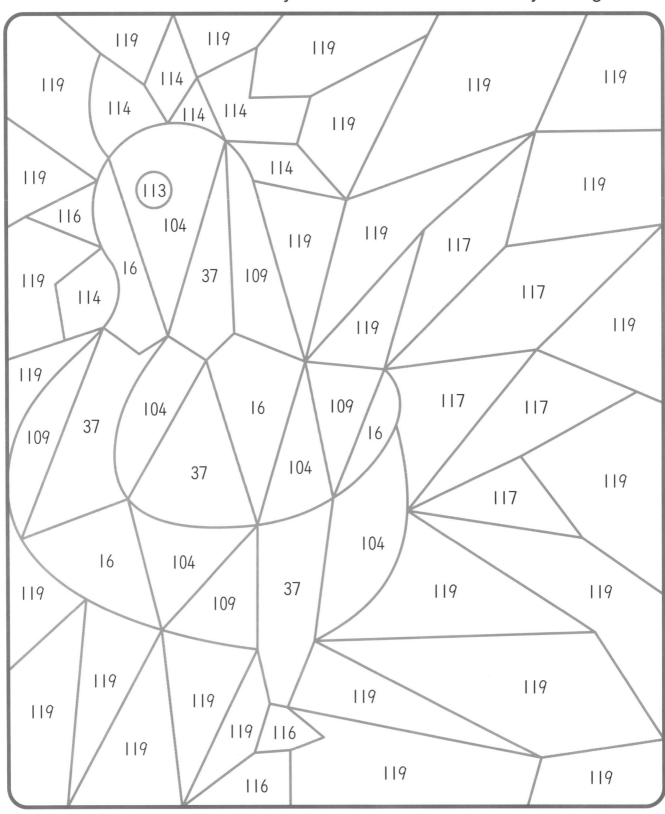

56

Ahoy, There!

■ Draw a line from 1 to 130 in order while saying each number.

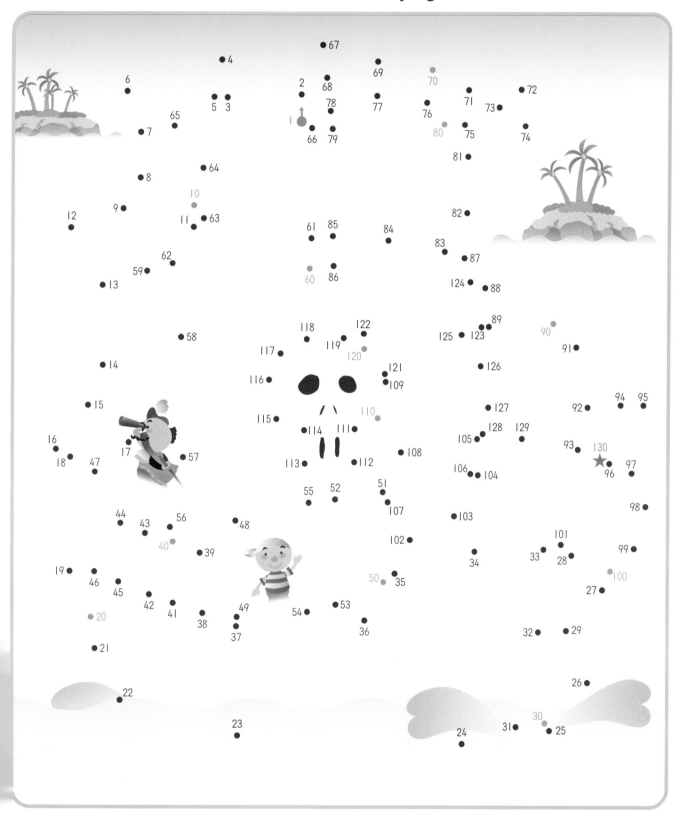

What Is It?

■ Use the key below to color by number.

121 = red   122 = yellow   123 = blue   124 = black   125 = yellow orange

127   129   122   122   125   127   127
126   126   125   128
129   128   125   129   126
127   126   125   128
126   128   127   125   128
129   125
129   121   122   121   126   129   125
127   123   123   121   128   126   125   127
126   125
123   121   121   121   125
123   121   125   121
125   125
121   121   121   122   121
121   125   125
121   124   129   126   124   121
121   121   121   124   124
128   122   122   122
126   124   128   126   124   128   124   127

58

Name

Date

■ Draw a line from 1 to 130 in order while saying each number.

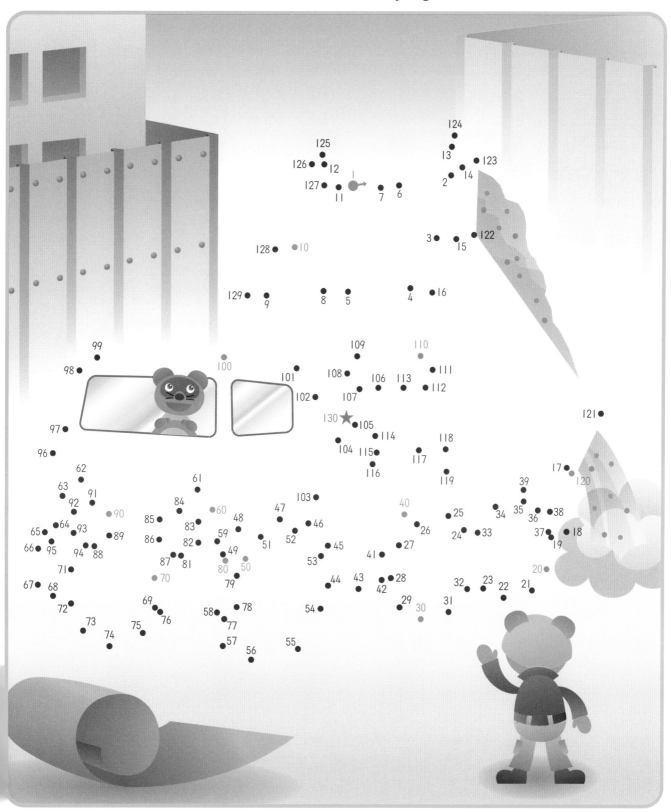

What Is It?

■ Use the key below to color by number.

125 = blue   126 = violet (purple)   127 = blue green   128 = brown
129 = green   130 = black

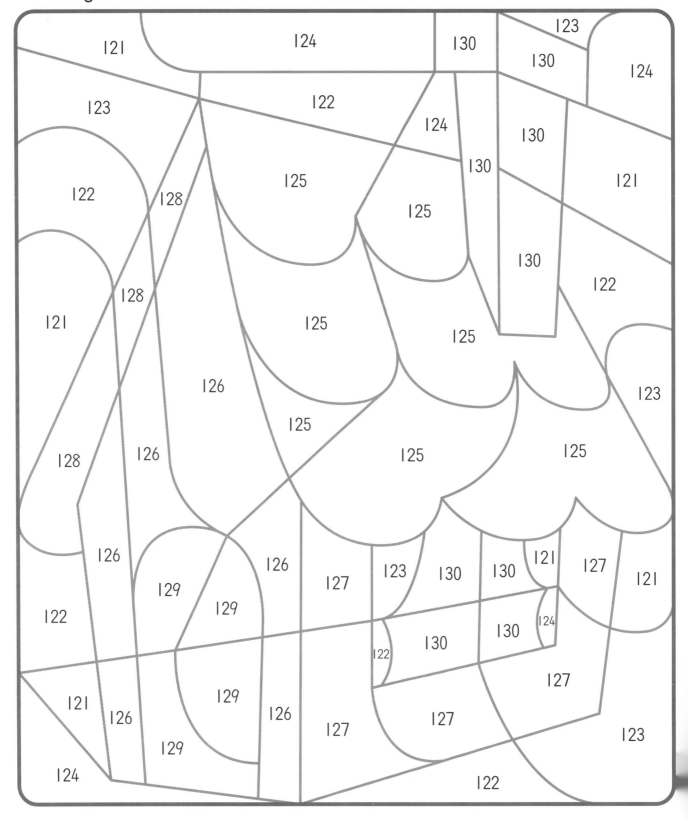

Name

Date

■ Draw a line from 1 to 130 in order while saying each number.

What Is It?

■ Use the key below to color by number.
121 = red violet   123 = orange   124 = blue green   126 = blue violet
129 = green   130 = blue

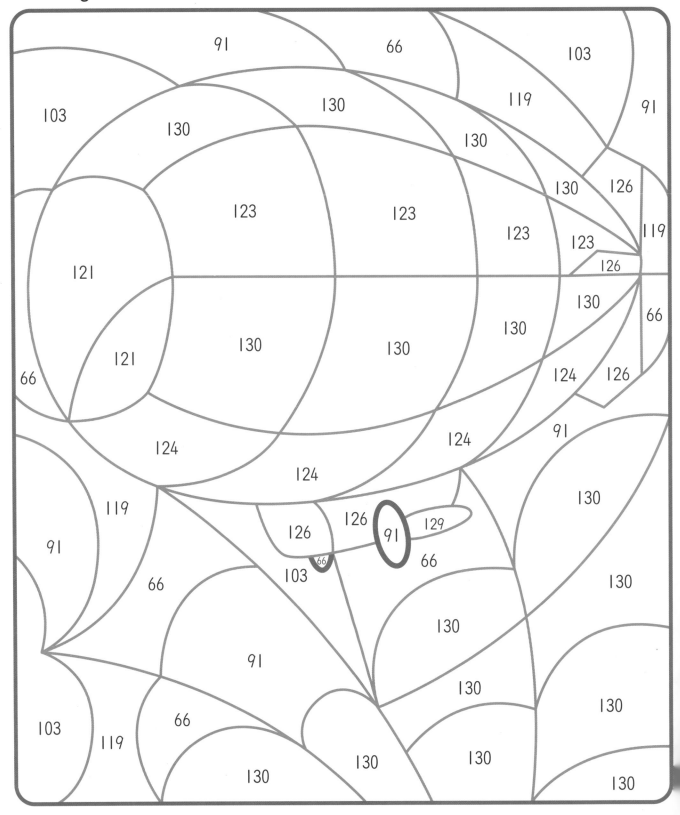

62

A Fine Day

To parents On this page, your child will have to draw many lines that cross other lines. If your child has difficulty finding the numbers, please point them out. Praise your child as he or she finishes each activity.

■ Draw a line from 1 to 130 in order while saying each number.

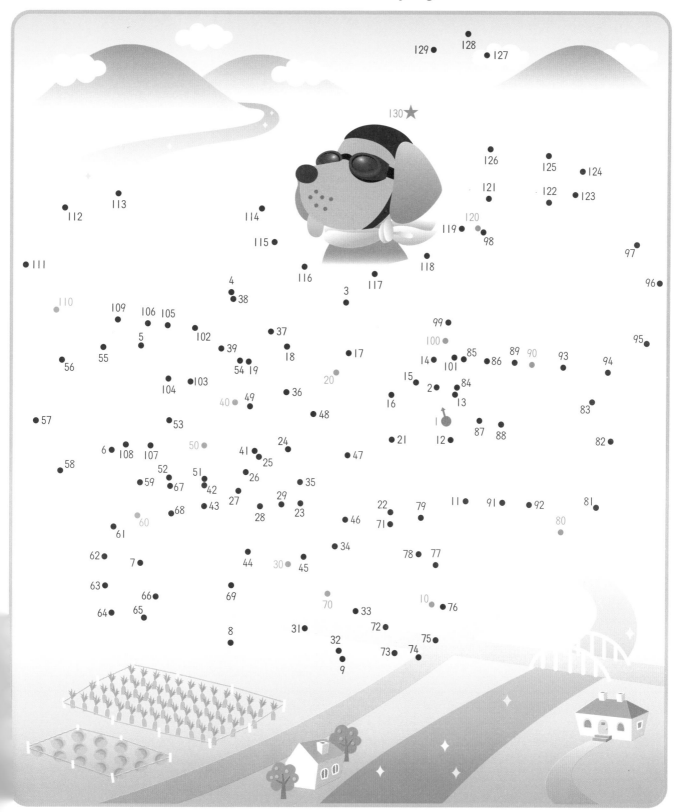

What Is It?

■ Use the key below to color by number.

122 = yellow   123 = blue violet   125 = blue   127 = black   128 = brown

130 = yellow orange

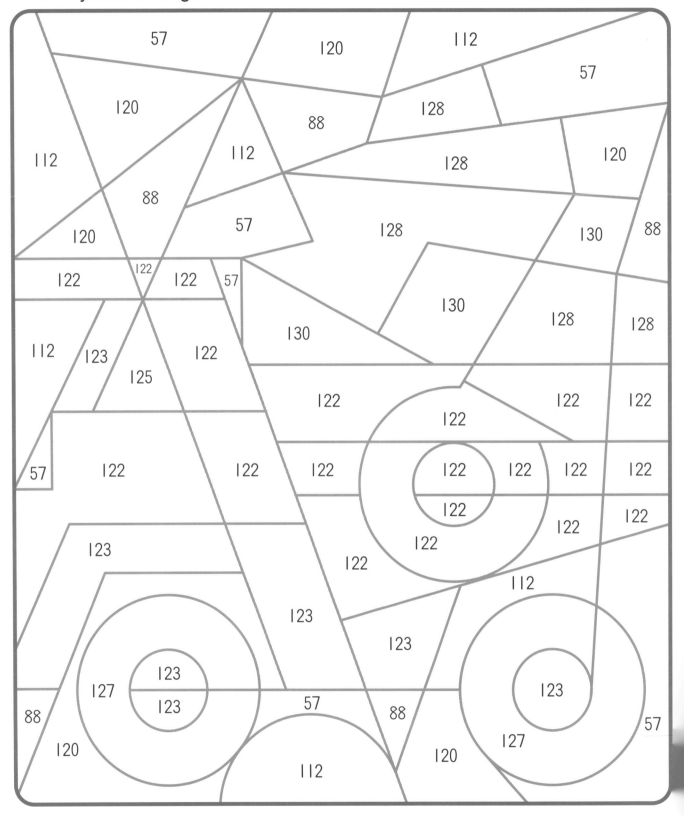

64

Chug Chug

■ Draw a line from 1 to 140 in order while saying each number.

What Is It?

■ Use the key below to color by number.

131 = orange   132 = yellow green   133 = black   134 = violet (purple)
135 = blue   136 = brown

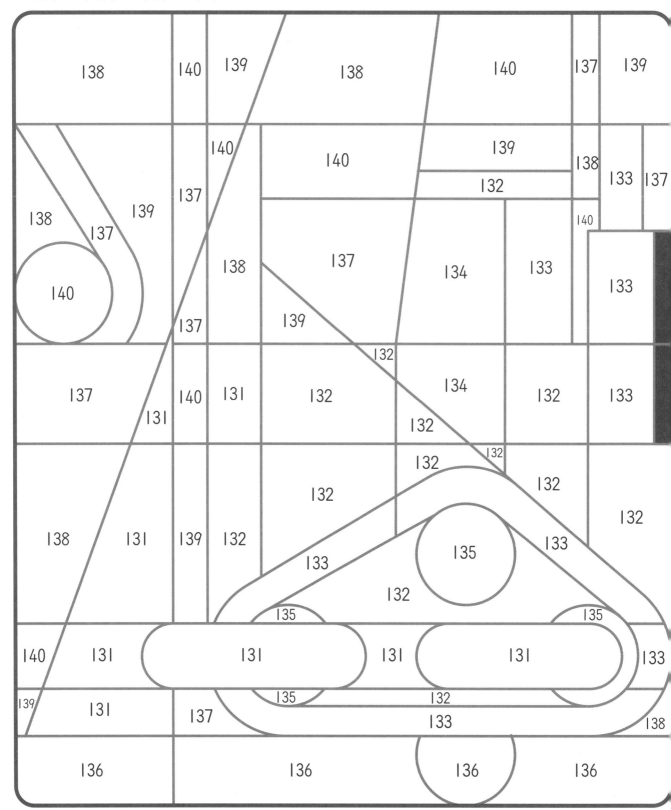

66

I Have Spiky Plates

■ Draw a line from 1 to 140 in order while saying each number.

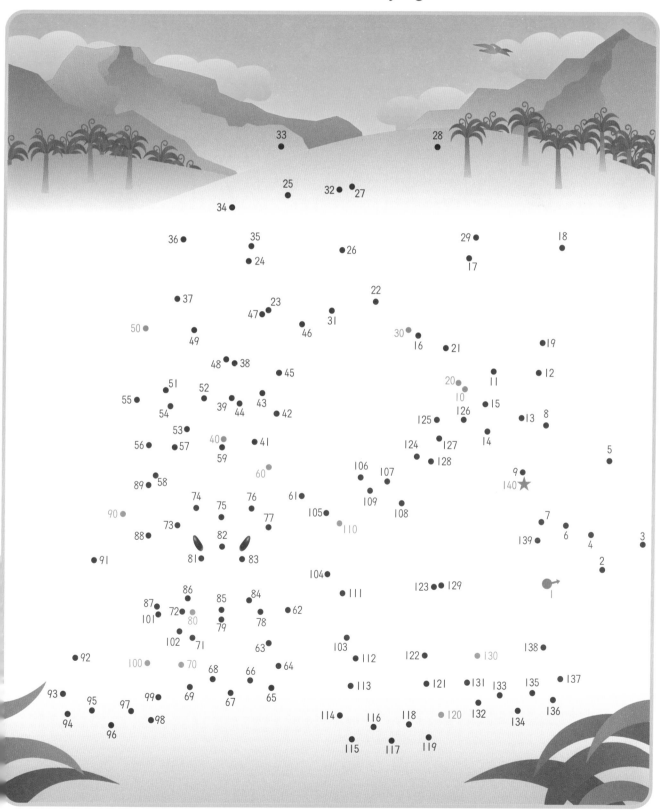

67

What Is It?

■ Use the key below to color by number.

135 = yellow   136 = blue   137 = orange   138 = carnation pink

139 = red   140 = red violet

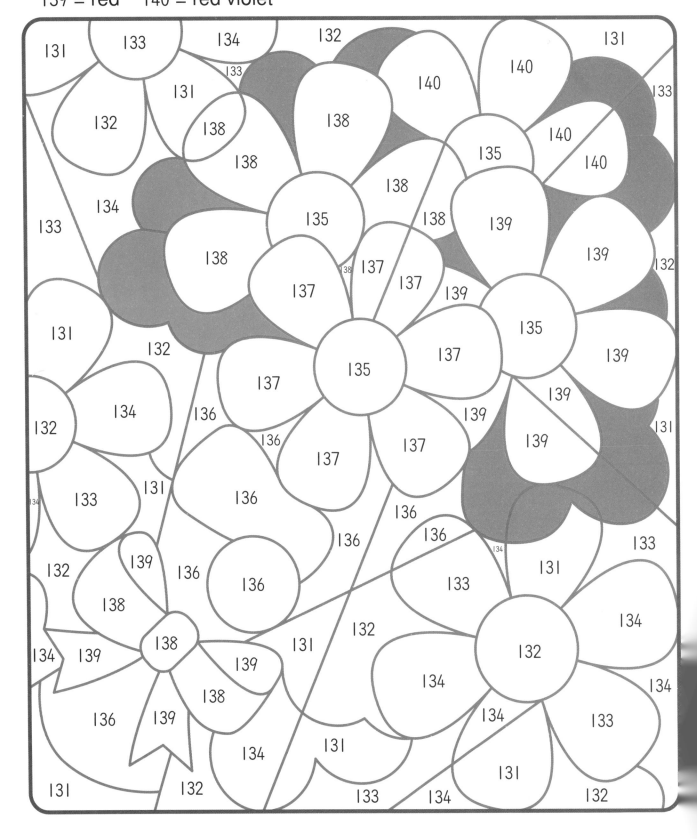

Name

Date

To parents On this page, your child will have to draw many lines that cross other lines. It may be difficult for him or her to draw straight lines especially when the next number is farther away. If your child has difficulty finding the numbers and drawing the lines, please offer to help.

■ Draw a line from 1 to 140 in order while saying each number.

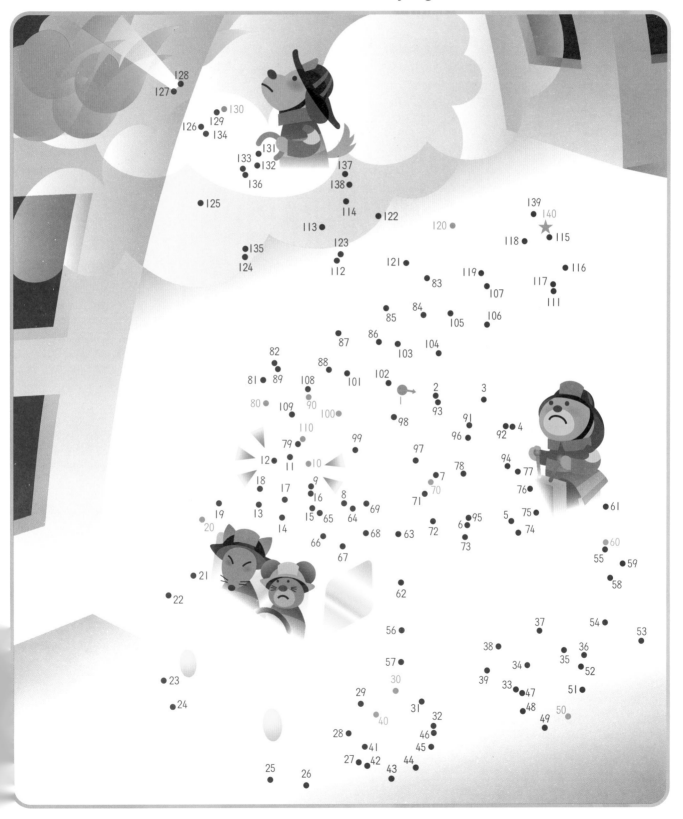

69

What Is It?

■ Use the key below to color by number.

131 = brown   132 = yellow orange   133 = red   134 = red violet

137 = carnation pink   139 = blue violet

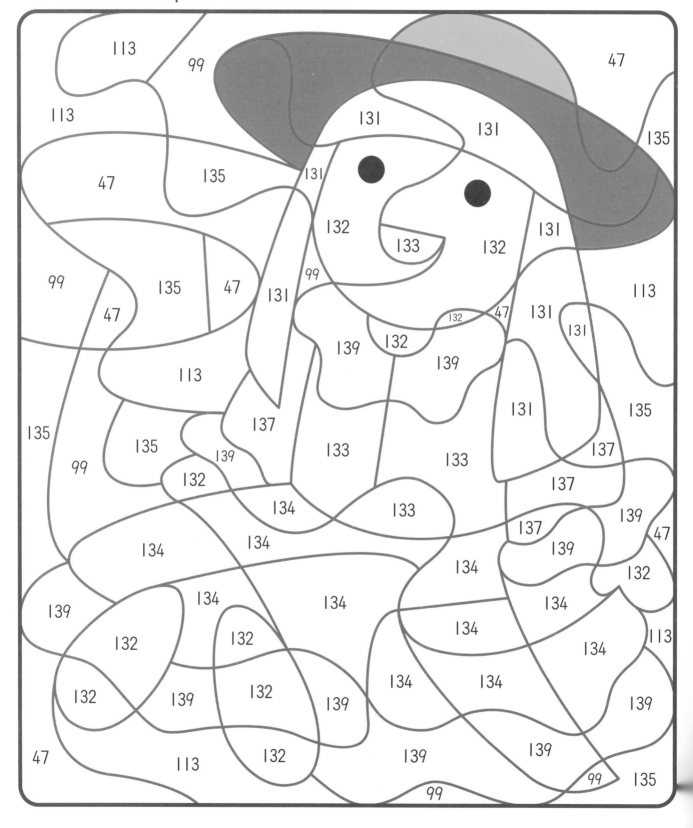

36 What Do You See?

Name

Date

■ Draw a line from 1 to 150 in order while saying each number.

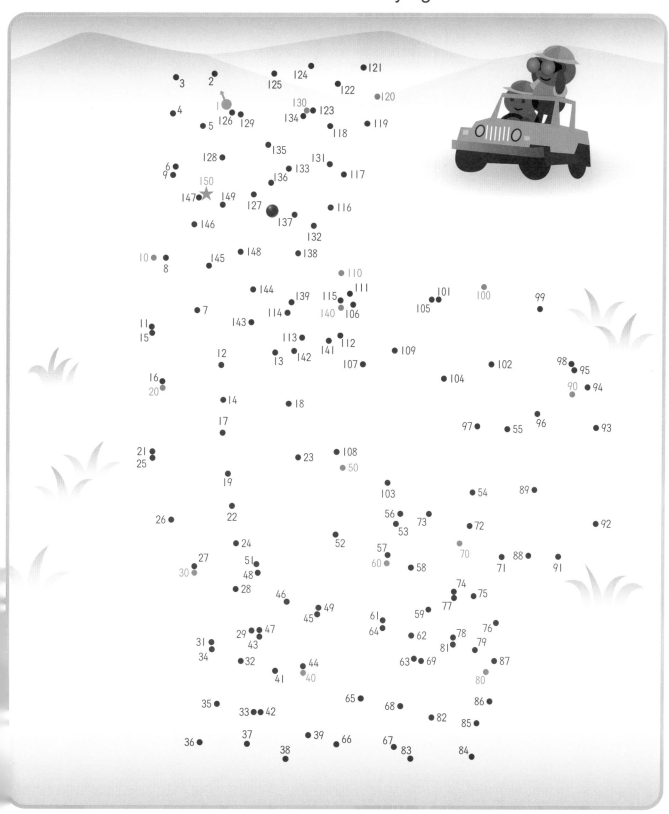

71

What Is It?

■ Use the key below to color by number.
141 = yellow   142 = red orange   143 = yellow green   144 = red violet
145 = violet (purple)   146 = brown   147 = blue

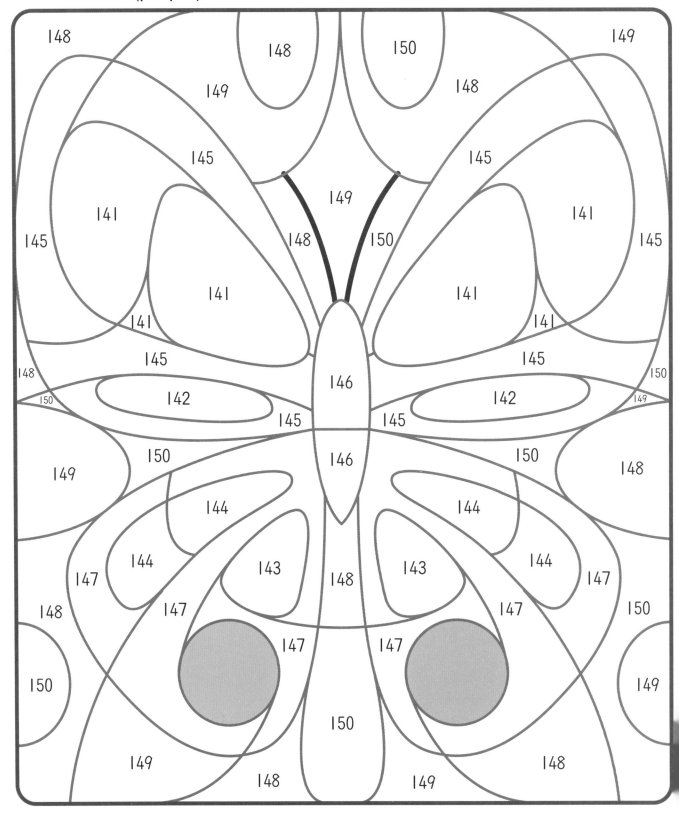

Name

Date

■ Draw a line from 1 to 150 in order while saying each number.

What Is It?

■ Use the key below to color by number.

144 = yellow   145 = carnation pink   146 = blue green   147 = green

148 = yellow green   149 = blue   150 = blue violet

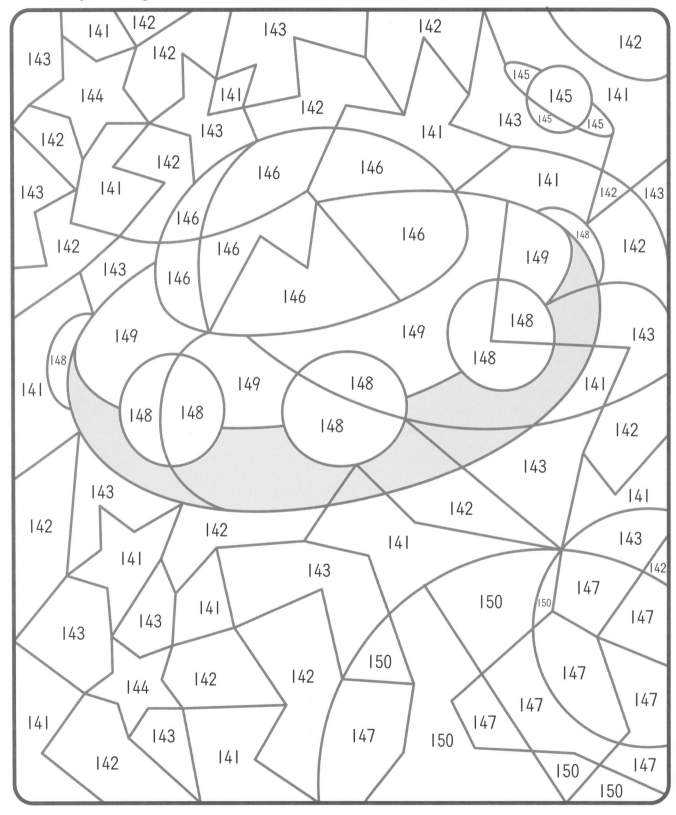

74

38 I Can Move Mountains

Name
Date

To parents On this page, your child will have to draw many lines that cross other lines. It may be difficult for him or her to draw straight lines especially when the next number is farther away. If your child has difficulty finding the numbers and drawing the lines, please offer to help. Give your child lots of praise for his or her effort!

■ Draw a line from 1 to 150 in order while saying each number.

75

What Is It?

■ Use the key below to color by number.

141 = black   142 = red orange   143 = orange   145 = blue

147 = blue green   148 = green   150 = yellow green

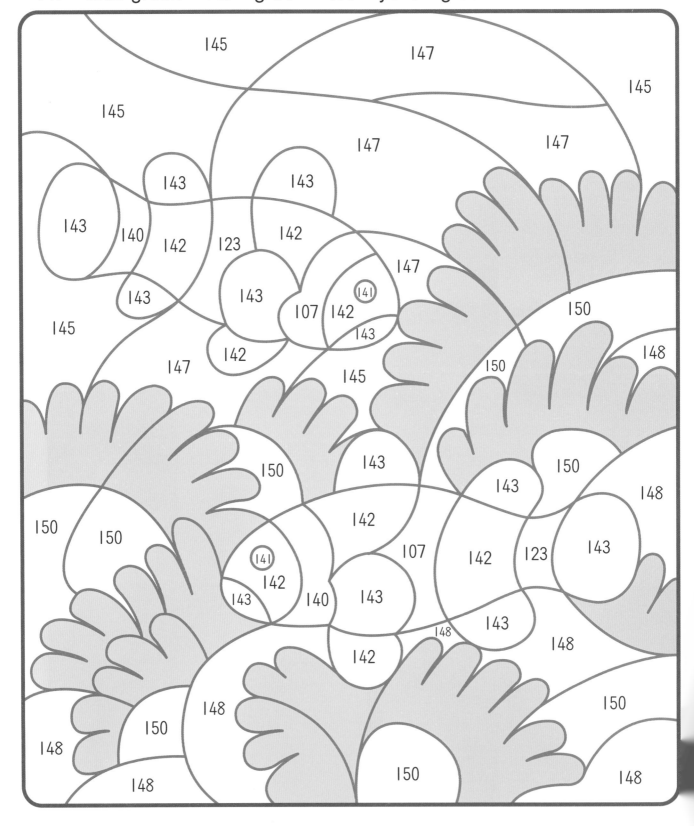

Answer Key

p. 1 chicken

p. 2 tomato

p. 3 dog

p. 4 scissors

p. 5 tugboat

p. 6 mitt and ball

p. 7 crocodile

p. 8 bag

p. 9 Triceratops

p. 10 lollipop

p. 11 submarine

p. 12 minibike

p. 13 walrus

p. 14 race car

p. 15 gorilla

p. 16 crab

p. 17 hornbill

p. 18 turtle

p. 19 sailing ship

p. 20 cat

Answer Key

p. 21 Tyrannosaurus

p. 22 swan

p. 23 passenger ship

p. 24 pineapple

p. 25 helicopter

p. 26 cup of tea

p. 27 ostrich

p. 28 lion

p. 29 parrot

p. 30 cactus

p. 31 giraffe

p. 32 fan

p. 33 chameleon

p. 34 balloon

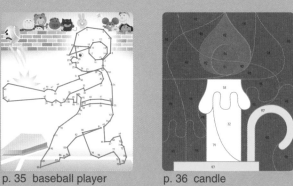

p. 35 baseball player

p. 36 candle

p. 37 eagle

p. 38 car

p. 39 lion

p. 40 teddy bear

Answer Key

p. 41 hippo

p. 42 whale

p. 43 lion

p. 44 helicopter

p. 45 cement mixer

p. 46 zebra

p. 47 classic car

p. 48 shoe

p. 49 duck and toy horse

p. 50 backhoe

p. 51 astronaut

p. 52 ship

p. 53 Santa Claus

p. 54 airplane

p. 55 genie

p. 56 chicken

p. 57 pirate ship

p. 58 fire engine

p. 59 dump truck

p. 60 house

79

Answer Key

p. 61 truck

p. 62 blimp

p. 63 biplane

p. 64 dump truck

p. 65 steam engine

p. 66 crawler loader

p. 67 Stegosaurus

p. 68 bouquet

p. 69 fire engine

p. 70 doll

p. 71 zebra

p. 72 butterfly

p. 73 tiger

p. 74 UFO

p. 75 bulldozer

p. 76 clown fish

KUMON

Certificate of Achievement

is hereby congratulated on completing

My Book of Number Games 1 - 150

Presented on _____ , 20 ___

_____
Parent or Guardian

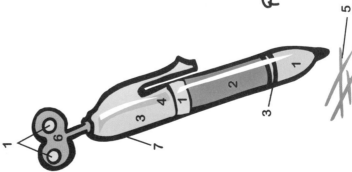

color-by-number

| 1 | 2 | 3 | 4 | 5 | 6 | 7 |